YAKS YAK

Animal Word Pairs

LINDA SUE PARK

ILLUSTRATED BY
JENNIFER BLACK REINHARDT

CLARION BOOKS
An Imprint of HarperCollinsPublishers

Yaks yak.

Bugs bug bugs.

Flounders flounder.

Quails quail.

to quail = to shrink away in fear

Apes ape.

to ape = to mimic

Dogs dog dogs.

to dog = to track or follow

Badgers badger.

Bats bat.

Cranes crane.

Rams ram.

Duck, ducks!

to duck = to crouch or dive

Steers steer.

Crows crow.

Kids kid!

to kid = to tease or joke

The word pairs used in this book are **homographs**—words that are spelled and pronounced the same, but have different meanings.

The Words

	ANIMAL'S NAME	ACTION
yak · to yak	From the Tibetan word for the animal, *g-yag*.	Probably onomatopoetic ("yakkety-yak"), possibly from the Yiddish *yakhne*, meaning busybody.
bug · to bug	Middle English *bugge*, something frightening, possibly related to the Scottish *bogill*, meaning goblin.	First use of *bug* meaning "to annoy or irritate" in the 1940s.
flounder · to flounder	Old North French, *flondre*.	Possibly a variation of *founder*, meaning to collapse or submerge. Also possible: from the Dutch *flodderen*, to flop around.
quail · to quail	From the Old French (*quaille*), or possibly a Germanic source (German *Wachtel*, Dutch *kwakkel*).	To shrink away in fear, from the mid-1500s; usage revived and popularized in the nineteenth century by Sir Walter Scott.
ape · to ape	Old English *apa*, meaning ape or monkey.	From the animal's behavior.
dog · to dog	Old English *docga*, Middle English *dogge*, meaning hound.	From the animal, as in to track or trail someone like a dog.
fish · to fish	Old English *fisc*.	From the animal.
badger · to badger	Possibly from the Anglo-French *bage*, meaning "badge," for the white blaze on its head.	From badger-baiting, a blood sport where dogs and badgers are pitted against each other for entertainment. Outlawed for nearly two centuries, but still practiced illegally in Britain and Ireland.
parrot · to parrot	Sixteenth century, uncertain origin. Possibly derived from the French *perroquet*, meaning parakeet.	From the bird's ability to mimic speech without understanding it.

The Words

	ANIMAL'S NAME	ACTION
bat · to bat	Middle English *bakke*, possibly later confused with the Latin *blatta* (meaning moth or other nocturnal insect).	To strike with a bat, from Old English *batt*, meaning a club or cudgel, the verb deriving from the noun.
slug · to slug	Middle English, from *sluggard*, a lazy or slow person (which in turn comes from Scandinavia: Norwegian *slugga*, Swedish *slogga*).	First use mid-1800s, uncertain origin.
crane · to crane	Old English *cran*, meaning a large wading bird.	From the bird's behavior.
ram · to ram	Old English *ramm*, meaning a male sheep.	From the animal's behavior.
duck · to duck	Old English *duce*, from the verb *ducan*, to duck or dive.	The meaning "to dive" from the bird's behavior. The variant definition "to stoop or bend quickly" first used in the sixteenth century.
steer · to steer	Old English *steor*, young bull.	Old English *steran*, meaning rudder.
crow · to crow	Old English *crawe*, imitating the bird's call.	From the bird's behavior, possibly because it is a carrion eater and squawks triumphantly over its feed.
hog · to hog	Old English *hocg* or *hogg*.	First recorded use 1884, in Mark Twain's *Huckleberry Finn*.
kid · to kid	Old Norse *kiδ*, meaning baby goat. First used to mean "child" in the sixteenth century.	Meaning "to tease or joke" first used mid-nineteenth century, probably from the idea of "acting like a kid."

To Tobin
who gave me the idea
—L.S.P.

Dedicated with love to EMR—your heart always remembers
—J.B.R.

HarperCollins Children's Books, a division of HarperCollins Publishers, 195 Broadway, New York, NY 10007

HarperCollins Publishers, Macken House, 39/40 Mayor Street Upper, Dublin 1, D01 C9W8, Ireland

Clarion Books is an imprint of HarperCollins Publishers.

Yaks Yak: Animal Word Pairs
Text copyright © 2016 by Linda Sue Park
Illustrations copyright © 2016 by Jennifer Black Reinhardt
All rights reserved. Manufactured in Capriate San Gervasio, Italy
No part of this book may be used or reproduced in any manner whatsoever without written permission except in the case of brief quotations embodied in critical articles and reviews. Without limiting the exclusive rights of any author, contributor, or the publisher of th s publication, any unauthorized use of this publication to train generative artificial intelligence (AI) technologies is expressly prohibited. HarperCollins also exercises their rights under Article 4(3) of the Digital Single Market Directive 2019/790 and expressly reserves this publication from the text and data mining exception.
www.harpercollins.com

Library of Congress Cataloging-in-Publication Data
Names: Park, Linda Sue. | Reinhardt, Jennifer Black, 1963 – illustrator.
Title: Yaks yak : animal word pairs / Linda Sue Park ; illustrated by Jennifer Black Reinhardt.
Description: Boston ; New York : Clarion Books, [2016] | Summary: Presents animals acting out the verbs made from their names, including hogs hogging, slugs slugging, and other creatures demonstrating homographs, words with different meanings that are spelled and pronounced the same.
Identifiers: LCCN 2015020003 | ISBN 9780544391017 (hardback) | ISBN 9780063484498 (paperback)
Subjects: | CYAC: English language —Homonyms — Fiction. | Animals — Fiction. | BISAC: JUVENILE FICTION / Concepts / Words. | JUVENILE FICTION / Animals / General. | JUVENILE FICTION / Humorous Stories.
Classification: LCC PZ7.P22115 Yak 2016 | DDC [E] — dc23
LC record available at http://lccn.loc.gov/2015020003

The artist used watercolor and ink on Arches 300 lb bright white, hot press, watercolor paper to create the illustrations for this book.
Typography by Christine Kettner
25 26 27 28 29 RTLO 10 9 8 7 6
First Edition